Oh, no... it's **The Moe & Joe Show!** ®

Moe: Say, Joe! What is your favorite book?

Joe: Well, Moe... The Mighty Big Book of Joe-kes!

MIGHTY BIG BOOK OF JOKES

DEDICATED to ALEX YOU ROCK!

LIBRARY OF CONGRESS CONTROL NUMBER: 2001091221

ISBN 978-0-8431-7582-0
11 12 13 14 15 16 17 18 19 20

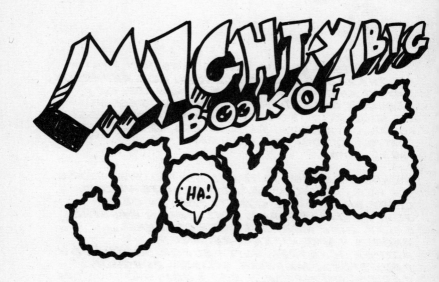

MIGHTY BIG BOOK OF JOKES

HA!

LIBRARY O' LAUGHS

PSS!
PRICE STERN SLOAN

THIS BOOK IS MANY PEOPLE'S BABY. FIRST A *BIG THANKS* TO *CLIZIA GUSSONI, JON ANDERSON, JAYNE ANTIPOW, PATRICIA PASQUALE,* AND *REBECCA GOLDBERG,* WHOSE WORK WAS ESSENTIAL TO THE SUCCESS OF THIS BOOK. IT INCLUDED NUMBERLESS ROUNDS OF PROOFREADING, SLEEPLESS NIGHTS, QUALITY CONTROL, COORDINATION, MANAGEMENT, WRITING AND REWRITING.

WE WOULD ALSO LIKE TO *THANK* THE FOLLOWING PEOPLE FOR THEIR HARD WORK: *TRACEY ARMISTO-VITOLO, CINDY BARRY, JOY COURT, DARREN CRUZ, JODI HUELIN, ROSALIE LENT, PAULA MAESTRO-SALAT, MIKE MARRO, LUKE MCDONNELL, ANGELA NAPOSKI, KRIS REINHOLD, ARTHUR SCHOEDEL, BETTY SOKOL, SCOTT SMITH, PAUL STONE, AVARELLE, VALISSA, DONOVAN, CARLOS,* AND ESPECIALLY *MOE & JOE,* WHO TOOK TIME FROM THEIR BUSY SCHEDULES TO APPEAR IN THESE PAGES!

What do you get when the equator is thankful?

Latitude gratitude!

A WISE MAN ONCE SAID, *"LAUGH* AND THE WORLD *LAUGHS* WITH YOU; *TRIP* AND THE *WORLD* LAUGHS *AT* YOU." OKAY, SO IT WASN'T A *WISE MAN* WHO SAID THAT, IT WAS *ME,* BUT IT STILL MAKES SENSE. IF *YOU LAUGH,* THE PERSON NEXT TO YOU WILL *GIGGLE,* AND THE PERSON NEXT TO THAT PERSON WILL *CHUCKLE,* AND BEFORE YOU KNOW IT EVERYONE AROUND YOU WILL BE *ROLLING ON THE FLOOR WITH LAUGHTER!*

TO HELP YOU SPREAD THE *JOY,* I'VE PACKED THIS BOOK FULL OF *SIDE-SPLITTERS* AND *GUT-BUSTERS* TO GET THE GIGGLES GOING. I'VE EVEN INCLUDED A STYLE OF JOKE I INVENTED ALL ON MY OWN... *RHYME TIME® JOKES!*

FOR *MORE* LAUGHS, VISIT *RIDDLES4KIDS.COM* AND YOU CAN GIVE US SOME OF *YOUR* OWN FUNNIES FOR OUR *NEXT* BOOK! *HA-HA!*
YOUR PAL,

CRAIG

CRAIG YOE

WHAT *TIME* WOULD IT BE IF *GODZILLA* CAME TO *SCHOOL?*

... TIME TO *RUN!*

HAT'S A *CHICKEN'S* FAVORITE *NURSERY RHYME?*

... "LITTLE BO *PEEP-PEEP!*"

What do you call a talkative taxi driver? A blabby cabby!

WHAT **SPORT** CAN **YOU** PLAY
WITH A **LOLLIPOP?**

... **SUCKER!**

OW DO **STINKY SOCKS** TALK TO
EACH OTHER?

... THEY CALL EACH OTHER ON
THE **SMELL-E-**PHONE!

What do you call an
indecisive infant?

A maybe baby!

WHERE DO **YOU** THROW **APPLE CORES** AFTER YOU'VE EATEN THE **APPLE?**

 ... IN A USED **CORE** LOT!

OW DID THE **PARAMEDIC** REVIVE THE **VEGETABLE?**

... HE USED C-**PEA**-R!

 HY DIDN'T **BATMAN** MARRY **CATWOMAN**?

... HE WANTED TO REMAIN A **BAT**-CHELOR!

WHAT HAPPENED WHEN THE **BLUE FAIRY** KISSED **PINOCCHIO**?

 ... SHE GOT **SPLINTERS** ON HER **LIPS**!

Oh, no... it's **The Moe & Joe Show!** ® *Moe*: Say, Joe! How did the flight attendant exercise?

 Joe: Well, Moe... she did air-robics!

WHAT DID THE **FLOWER CHILD** ORDER
AT **McDONALD'S?**

... A **HIPPY** MEAL!

WHAT DO **YOU** CALL A **DANCE** WHERE
YOU GET TO **KNOW BUTCHERS?**

... A **MEAT** BALL!

What do you call an
HBO movie?

A cable fable!

WHY SHOULDN'T *YOU* *MOW* THE *LAWN* WITH A *SMILE?*

... IT'S BETTER TO USE A *LAWNMOWER!*

WHAT DO *YOU* CALL *DECIDING* WHETHER TO WATCH *CNN* OR *CNBC?*

... *PICKING* YOUR *NEWS!*

WHAT DO *YOU* GET WHEN YOU CROSS *BUGS BUNNY* WITH *KERMIT THE FROG?*

... A *BUNNY RIBBIT!*

Oh, no... it's **The Moe & Joe Show!** ® *Moe:* Say, Joe! What does a fisherman do in a fire?

  Joe: Well, Moe... stop, drop and reel!

WHY DID THE *ELEPHANT* GET *FIRED* FROM HIS *COMPUTER JOB*?

... BECAUSE HE WAS AFRAID OF THE *MOUSE*!

WHAT *SITS* BY YOUR *BED* AT NIGHT WITH ITS *TONGUE* HANGING OUT?

... A *SHOE*!

What do you call the Trojan Horse? A phony pony!

HOW DO **YOU** MAKE A **PIANO LAUGH?**

... TICKLE ITS **IVORIES!**

What do you call a bird that belongs to Noah?

An ark lark!

Oh, no... it's **The Moe & Joe Show!** ® Moe: Say, Joe! What do you always overlook?

 Joe: Well, Moe... your nose!

CITY SNICKERS DEPARTMENT

WHAT CITY **WANDERS AROUND** AIMLESSLY?

(**ROME!**)

WHAT CITY HAS THE **MOST EMPLOYERS?**

(**BOSS**-TON!)

HAT CITY HAS **TWO** OF **EVERTHING?**

(**PAIR**-IS!)

WHAT CITY **EATS** THE **MOST CHERRIES?**

(**PITTS**-BURGH!)

WHAT CITY HAS THE **MOST ROWBOATS?**

(**OAR**-LANDO!)

WHAT CITY HAS THE **MOST BABY CHICKENS** IN IT?

CHICK-AGO!

WHAT IS THE **WEALTHIEST CITY?**

RICH-MOND!

WHAT CITY IS **TILTED?**

NEW OR-**LEANS!**

WHAT CITY **MOOS?**

MOS-**COW!**

WHAT CITY HAS THE **BEST EYESIGHT?**

SEE-ATTLE!

HAT CITY IS ALWAYS **ANGRY?**

MAD-ISON!

WHAT CITY IS **REALLY ODD?**

ALBU-**QUIRKY!**

WHAT CITY HAS THE **MOST MATTRESSES?**

PALM-**SPRINGS!**

WHICH CITY IS **VERY FRIENDLY?**

NICE!

WHAT CITY **LENDS OUT** A LOT OF **MONEY?**

BARCE-**LOAN**-A!

WHAT DID THE **GARBAGE COLLECTOR'S MOTHER** SAY?

 ... "QUIT TALKING **TRASH!**"

 HAT'S **ROUND** AND **GREEN** AND WINS **BEAUTY CONTESTS?**

... PRETTY **PEAS!**

 What do you call a farting dog?

A gassy Lassie!

HAT'S **BLACK** AND **WHITE** AND **YELLOW** AND **GREEN?**

... A TAXI-**CABBAGE!**

WHEN CAN **YOU** MOVE AS **FAST** AS A **HORSE?**

 ... WHEN **YOU'RE ON ONE!**

WHERE DOES **SNOW WHITE** KEEP HER **CLOTHES?**

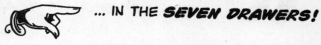 ... IN THE **SEVEN DRAWERS!**

 What do you call a top scholar? A main brain!

WHAT DO *YOU* CALL A *JOKE* ABOUT *BREAD?*

... A BREAD *SCHTICK!*

HAT DO *YOU* CALL A *GOOSE* STANDING ON ITS *HEAD?*

... UPSIDE *DOWN!*

What do you call a happy father? A glad dad!

WHY DO **POTATOES** MAKE GOOD **DETECTIVES?**
... BECAUSE THEY KEEP THEIR **EYES PEELED!**

 HAT DOES A **SKELETON** SAY WHEN STARTING **DINNER?**
... "**BONE** APPETIT!"

Oh, no... it's **The Moe & Joe Show!** ®   *Moe*: Say, Joe! What fruit does a sheep like?

 Joe: Well, Moe... baa-nanas!

WHERE DO *ZOMBIES* LIVE?

... ON *DEAD-END* STREETS!

WHAT DO *YOU* CALL A *BOOMERANG'S KID?*
... A *BABY BOOMER*-ANG!

What do you call a big bottom?

A plump rump!

GARY: WHAT DO *YOU* CALL A VERY STINKY *CLEANING FLUID?*
MARY: *AMMONIA* GONNA TELL YOU THE ANSWER ONE TIME!

WHAT DO *YOU* GET WHEN YOU CROSS A *CAR WINDOW* WITH A *HAMBURGER?*

... *WINDSHIELD WHOPPERS!*

HOW DOES A *FAIRY TALE* ABOUT *FROGS* END?

... "THEY LIVED *HOPPILY* EVER AFTER!"

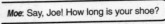
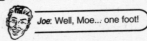

WHY DIDN'T THE **NOSE** MAKE THE **SOCCER TEAM?**

... HE DIDN'T GET **PICKED!**

What do you call Dracula's accent?

Fang twang!

What do you call a
fast horse?

A speed steed!

WHERE DOES A *TREE* DO ITS *BANKING?*

... AT A *BRANCH* OFFICE!

WHAT IS THE *MOST SHOCKING STORY* IN THE *HISTORY BOOKS?*

... WHEN BEN FRANKLIN DISCOVERED *ELECTRICITY!*

WHAT DOES AN *ELEPHANT* CALL HIS *FATHER'S SISTER?*

... ELEPH-*AUNT!*

Oh, no... it's **The Moe & Joe Show!** ®

 Moe: Say, Joe! What kind of ears do trains have?

 Joe: Well, Moe... engine-ears!

HY DOES *TIGER WOODS* WEAR *TWO PAIRS* OF *PANTS?*

... IN CASE HE GETS A *HOLE IN ONE!*

WHAT IS *BLACK* AND *WHITE* AND *GOES UP* AND *DOWN?*

 ... A *ZEBRA* IN AN *ELEVATOR!*

WHERE DOES *SUNDAY* COME AFTER *MONDAY?*

... IN THE *DICTIONARY!*

WHAT'S THE *DIFFERENCE* BETWEEN *HERE* AND *THERE*?

... THE LETTER *"T!"*

WHY SHOULDN'T *YOU* DO *HOMEWORK* ON AN *EMPTY STOMACH*?

... IT'S BETTER TO DO IT ON A *COMPUTER!*

What do you call a play acted by South American animals?

A llama drama!

WHAT DOES A **GHOST** WEAR IN THE **RAIN?**

... **BOOO**-TS!

WHAT DID THE **WATER BOY** ASK THE **BASEBALL TEAM?**

... "WHO'S ON **THIRST?"**

What do you call a cowboy joke?

A west jest!

WHAT DID THE **BRIDE OF FRANKENSTEIN** PUT ON HER **FACE**?

... **COVER GHOUL** MAKE-UP!

WHY DIDN'T **CATWOMAN** KISS **BRUCE WAYNE**?

... HE HAD **BAT** BREATH!

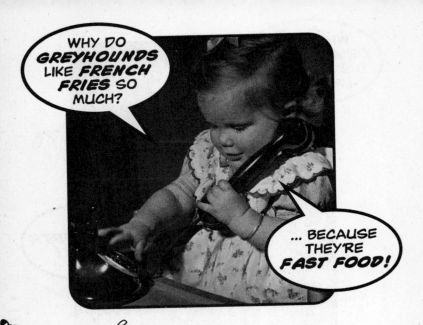

WHAT IS *RED, GROWS* ON *TREES,* AND HAS *PURPLE WHEELS*?

... AN *APPLE.* I LIED ABOUT THE *WHEELS!*

WHAT DO *YOU* CALL *FROSTY THE SNOWMAN* IN *JULY?*

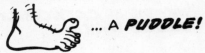 ... A *PUDDLE!*

WHERE DOES THE *FISHERMAN* CLEAN HIS *FISH?*

... IN THE *FISH-WASHING MACHINE!*

RHYME TIME!

What do you call a smashed penny?

A bent cent!

WHICH *VCR BUTTON* DOES A *CAT* LIKE TO *PRESS?*
... THE *PAWS BUTTON!*

WHAT *MUPPET* IS THE BEST *FOOTBALL PLAYER?*
... *TACKLE ME ELMO!*

Where does Mickey live?

In a mouse house!

WHAT HOLDS *WATER* EVEN THOUGH IT'S FULL OF *HOLES?*

... A *SPONGE!*

WHAT DO A *BANANA* AND A *RHINO* HAVE IN *COMMON?*

 ... THEY'RE BOTH *YELLOW* EXCEPT FOR THE *RHINO!*

Oh, no... it's **The Moe & Joe Show!** ® *Moe:* Say, Joe! What type of music do you hear in a cave?

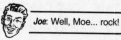 *Joe:* Well, Moe... rock!

Oh, no... it's **The Moe & Joe Show!** ® *Moe*: Say, Joe! Where are snacks served to football players?

Joe: Well, Moe... in the soup-er bowl!

WHAT DOES THE *MAMA WOLF* SAY TO THE *BABY WOLF* AT *NIGHTTIME?*

... "GO TO *SHEEP*, NOW!"

WHAT KIND OF *CARD* DO YOU SEND TO A *SHEPHERD?*

... A *GET WOOL* CARD!

WHY DID THE *HOCKEY PLAYER* GO TO THE *ORTHODONTIST?*

... BECAUSE HE HAD *PUCK TEETH!*

WHAT GOES "KRAB! KRAB!"?

... A DOG BARKING BACKWARDS!

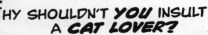

WHY SHOULDN'T *YOU* INSULT A *CAT LOVER?*

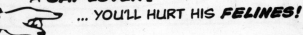

... YOU'LL HURT HIS *FELINES!*

RHYME TIME!

What do you call a magician's wand? A trick stick!

WHAT KIND OF **CLOTHES** DO **ATTORNEYS** WEAR?

 ... **LAW**-SUITS!

HAT DID THE **TREE** GET HIS **GIRLFRIEND** FOR HER **BIRTHDAY?**

... A **FIR** COAT!

Oh, no... it's **The Moe & Joe Show!** ® **Moe**: Say, Joe! What is a seamstress' favorite food?

 Joe: Well, Moe... hem-burgers!

 HAT *SOUND* DO *PORCUPINES* MAKE WHEN THEY *KISS?*

... *"SMACK! OUCH!"*

WHY DID THE *POTATOES* HAVE AN *ARGUMENT?*

... THEY COULDN'T SEE *EYE* TO *EYE!*

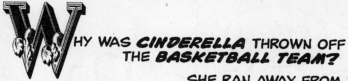

WHY WAS *CINDERELLA* THROWN OFF THE *BASKETBALL TEAM?*

... SHE RAN AWAY FROM THE *BALL.*

WHAT DID THE *POPSICLE* CALL HIS *FATHER'S SISTER?*

... AUNTY *FREEZE!*

What do you call good news?

A cheerful earful!

WHAT DO **YOU** GET WHEN YOU CROSS A **ROMAN EMPEROR** WITH A PAIR OF **SHEARS?**

... JULIUS **SCISSORS!**

What do you call a drama coach?

A speech teach!

HOW DID THE *FLEA* GET FROM *LOS ANGELES* TO *NEW YORK?*

... HE TOOK A *GREYHOUND!*

WHERE DO *YOU* GET *EXTRA CREDIT* FOR PASSING *NOTES* AT *SCHOOL?*

... IN *MUSIC CLASS!*

Oh, no... it's **The Moe & Joe Show!** ® *Moe*: Say, Joe! Why did the campfire go to the doctor?

 Joe: Well, Moe... he had glowing pains!

WHAT DOES *SUPERMAN* USE TO *WAKE UP* IN THE *MORNING?*

 ... AN ALARM *CLARK!*

HAT DID THE *CELERY* SAY TO THE *RADISH* AT THE *DANCE?*

... *"TURNIP* THE MUSIC!"

WHY DO *GIRL CAMELS* WEAR
PINK UNDERWEAR?

... TO TELL THEM APART FROM *BOY CAMELS!*

DEKE: WHAT'S THE *FIRST NAME* OF THE GUY
WHO DISCOVERED *ELECTRICITY?*
ZEKE: BEN WONDERING THAT MYSELF!

ZIP: WHAT *SLAM DUNKS* AND IS *FIERCE*
AND *BLUE?*
ZAP: THE *MICHAEL JORDAN RIVER!*

What do you call
a rainbow?

A hue view!

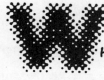 HAT'S *BLACK* AND *WHITE* AND *RED* ALL OVER THE *BOTTOM?*

... A *ZEBRA* WITH *DIAPER RASH!*

WHAT DOES A *PICKLE* SAY WHEN HE WANTS TO PLAY *CRAZY 8'S?*

 ... "*DILL* ME IN!"

 Oh, no... it's **The Moe & Joe Show!** ® *Moe:* Say, Joe! What's green and goes up and down?

 Joe: Well, Moe... a pickle on a see-saw!

WHAT DOES A *CHICKEN* EAT AT THE *MOVIES?*

 ... *PEEP*-CORN!

ROB: WHICH IS *BABY ELTON JOHN'S* MOST
FAMOUS *SONG?*
BOB: "*CRADLE IN THE WIND*"!

 Oh, no... it's The Moe & Joe Show! ® *Moe:* Say, Joe! What do you call half a tuba?

 Joe: Well, Moe... a one-ba!

WHY DID THE **SOLDIER** SALUTE THE **REFRIGERATOR**?

... BECAUSE IT WAS **GENERAL ELECTRIC!**

What do you call a magenta colored string?

A red thread!

HAT DID ONE **TONSIL** SAY TO THE OTHER **TONSIL?**

... "GET DRESSED, THE **DOC'S** TAKING US **OUT** TONIGHT!"

WHAT GOES **ACROSS** THE **COUNTRY** BUT STAYS IN A **CORNER?**

 ... A **STAMP!**

WHAT DO *YOU* CALL A *COUNTRY* THAT GIVES A LOT OF *TESTS?*

... AN *EXAM-I-NATION!*

What do you call
a gentle baby?

A mild child!

**W**HAT *TWO THINGS* CAN *YOU* NOT EAT FOR *BREAKFAST?*

... *LUNCH* AND *DINNER!*

HOW DO *BEES* GREET *EACH OTHER?*

... WITH A *HIVE FIVE!*

HOW DOES *DRACULA* LIKE HIS *COFFEE?*

 ... DE-*COFFIN*-ATED!

Oh, no... it's **The Moe & Joe Show!** ® *Moe*: Say, Joe! Why do rhinos have flat feet?

 Joe: Well, Moe... from jumping out of airplanes!

WHY DID THE **GORILLAS** CLOSE THEIR **LAW FIRM?**

 ... BECAUSE THEY ONLY GOT **MONKEY BUSINESS!**

HY DID THE **CHICKEN** CROSS THE **PLAYGROUND?**

... TO GET TO THE **OTHER SLIDE!**

WHAT **NURSERY RHYME** DO **GHOSTS** LOVE THE MOST?

... "LITTLE **BOO** PEEP!"

What do you call a fat hog?

A big pig!

WHAT DO **YOU** CALL SOMEONE WHO SHOWS UP FOR **WORK** IN A **ROBE?**

... A **JUDGE!**

HELLO, MAY I SPEAK TO **MR.** OR **MRS. WALL** PLEASE?

I'M SORRY, THERE ARE NO **WALLS** HERE.

THEN WHAT'S **HOLDING UP** YOUR **HOUSE?**

 **W**HAT DID THE *SHEEP* HAVE ON ITS *13TH BIRTHDAY?*

... A *BAA*-MITZVAH!

WHAT IS A *CAT'S* FAVORITE *TOY?*
... A *HAIR-BALL!*

What do you call a tool in prison?

A slammer hammer!

WHAT *REPTILE* IS GOOD TO HAVE
AROUND ON *MOVING DAY?*

... A *BOX TURTLE!*

WHY DID THE *CHICKEN* SIGN UP
FOR *BAND PRACTICE?*

... SHE WANTED TO USE
HER *DRUMSTICKS!*

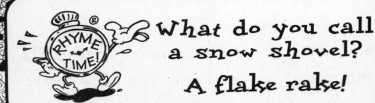

RHYME TIME!®

What do you call
a snow shovel?

A flake rake!

PAM: HAVE **YOU** HEARD ABOUT THE **COW** THAT DOESN'T GIVE **MILK**?
SAM: YUP, SHE'S A **MILK DUD**!

FRED: I KNOW A **MAN** WITH A **WOODEN LEG** NAMED **SMITH**.
NED: WHAT'S THE **NAME** OF HIS **OTHER LEG**?

Oh, no... it's **The Moe & Joe Show!** ® *Moe:* Say, Joe! What can't be used until it's broken?

 Joe: Well, Moe... an egg!

WHAT DO **YOU** GET WHEN YOU PUT **TOO MUCH MOUSSE** ON YOUR **HEAD?**

... **ANTLERS!**

WHY DIDN'T THE **SKELETON** DO HER **HOMEWORK?**

... SHE WAS A **LAZYBONE!**

What do you call a Sunday in Spring?

A May day!

WHAT DO **RAIN CLOUDS** WEAR?
... **THUNDER**-WEAR!

HY DON'T **SEAGULLS** FLY OVER
A **BAY?**

... 'CAUSE THEN YOU'D HAVE
TO CALL THEM **BAY-GULLS!**

What do you call the
thick border around
a house?

A dense fence!

BILL: DO *YOU* HAVE *HOLES* IN YOUR *SOCKS?*
LIL: NO, I *DON'T!*
BILL: WELL, HOW DO YOU GET YOUR
FEET INTO THEM?

HOW DO *YOU* KNOW THAT A *CLOCK* IS *HUNGRY?*

... IT GOES BACK FOR *SECONDS!*

Oh, no... it's **The Moe & Joe Show!** ® *Moe*: Say, Joe! Who is a cow's best friend?

 Joe: Well, Moe... a moo-se!

HICH **RAN FURTHEST** — THE **HAMBURGER** OR THE **HOT DOG?**

...THE FRANK **FURTHER!**

WHAT DOES **DRACULA** HAVE IN COMMON WITH A **VEGETARIAN?**

... HE CONSIDERS A **STAKE** HAZARDOUS TO HIS **HEALTH!**

WHAT DO **YOU** GET WHEN YOU CROSS A **PORCUPINE** WITH A **BALLOON?**

... **POP!**

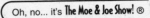

WHAT *TREE* DOES A *BEAR* LIKE TO *CLIMB?*

... A *FUR* TREE!

WHAT KIND OF A *MAN* CAN HOLD UP A *50-TON TRUCK* WITH *ONE HAND?*

... A *POLICEMAN!*

What do you call a haunted tent?

A creepy teepee!

WHAT HAPPENED TO THE *EXTREMELY HAIRY MAN* WHO WALKED INTO THE *WOODS?*
... *BIGFOOT* TOOK PICTURES OF *HIM!*

OW DO *YOU* CALL A *DOG* WITH *NO LEGS?*
... WHO CARES, HE *WON'T COME* ANYWAY!

Oh, no... it's **The Moe & Joe Show!** ® *Moe:* Say, Joe! What does a bat need in order to run?

 Joe: Well, Moe... a bat-tery!

WHICH **SIDE** OF A **DOG** HAS MORE **HAIR?**

... THE **OUT**-SIDE

WHAT DO **YOU** GET WHEN YOU CROSS A **BIG CAT** WITH A **NEWSPAPER?**

... A **HEAD-LION!**

CLAUDE: IF YOU HAVE **20 APPLES** IN **ONE HAND** AND **17** IN THE **OTHER,** WHAT DO YOU HAVE?

MAUDE: EITHER REALLY **BIG HANDS** OR REALLY **SMALL APPLES!**

Oh, no... it's **The Moe & Joe Show!** ® *Moe*: Say, Joe! How do vegetables keep in touch?

 Joe: Well, Moe... they use pea-mail!

WHAT IS A *DOG'S* FAVORITE *FOOD?*
... ANYTHING ON *YOUR* PLATE!

What do you call
a container filled
with ants?

A bug jug!

 HY WASN'T *BATMAN* ABLE TO *CATCH* ANY *FISH?*

... *ROBIN* ATE ALL THE *WORMS!*

WHAT DO *YOU* CALL A *BORING DINOSAUR?*

 ... A DINO-*SNORE!*

Oh, no... it's **The Moe & Joe Show!** ® **Moe**: Say, Joe! Why did the orange stop?

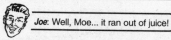 **Joe**: Well, Moe... it ran out of juice!

BAMBI: WHERE DO *FAIRIES* STORE THEIR *GOLD DUST?*
CANDY: IN THE *TREE TRUNK!*

WHAT DO *YOU* CALL SOMEONE WHO ANSWERS *PHONES* FOR A *FOOT?*

... A *SOCK-* RETARY!

LOU: ARE *YOU* GONNA GET A *TATTOO?*
STU: I'M GONNA *INK* ABOUT IT!

WHY DIDN'T THE *ZOMBIE* GO TO *SCHOOL?*

... HE WAS FEELING *ROTTEN!*

OW DO *YOU* MAKE A *TISSUE DANCE?*

... YOU PUT A LITTLE *BOOGIE* IN IT!

What do you call the Loch Ness monster?

A lake snake!

 HAT'S *YELLOW, CUDDLY,* AND *REALLY SMELLY?*

... WINNIE THE *P.U.!*

PATIENT: WHY DO I HAVE TO *WAKE UP* NOW?
NURSE: IT'S TIME FOR YOUR *SLEEPING PILL!*

Oh, no... it's **The Moe & Joe Show!** ® *Moe*: Say, Joe! What do you call an art contest judge?

 Joe: Well, Moe... an art-official!

WHO IS THE *SWEETEST DENTIST?*

... THE ONE WHO GIVES *CHOCOLATE FILLINGS!*

HY DON'T *YOU* WANT TO *EAT UP* THE *STREET?*

... I DON'T LIKE THE *TASTE* OF *CEMENT!*

SUE: WHERE DID *YOU* GET THAT *FURRY BANDAGE?*
LOU: FROM THE *FIRST AID KIT-TEN!*

Oh, no... it's **The Moe & Joe Show!** ® *Moe:* Say, Joe! What do you call a non-skid pancake?

 Joe: Well, Moe... a waffle!

 **HY DO *YOU* WANT THE *RAIN* TO *KEEP UP*?**

... BECAUSE THEN IT WON'T COME *DOWN!*

WHAT DO *YOU* TELL A *SELFISH SHEEP*?

... "IT'S NOT ALL ABOUT *EWE!*"

What do you call a bull fight?

A cattle battle!

WHY DID THE **POLICEMAN** ARREST THE **SLEEPING BABY?**

... FOR KID-**NAPPING!**

RHYME TIME!

What do you call a hunter?

A doe foe!

ALICIA: WHAT WOULD *YOU* DO IF YOU WERE IN *MY SHOES?*
FELICIA: POLISH THEM!

WHAT DOES A *DOG* HATE ON HIS *PIZZA?*

... MOZZARELLA *FLEAS!*

WHAT *BIRD* WOULD COME *IN HANDY* DURING *BOXING MATCHES?*

 ... A DUCK!

WHY DID THE **TONGUE** STAY UP **LATE?**

... BECAUSE HE WAS CRAMMING FOR HIS **TASTE TEST!**

WHAT **BUG** LIKES TO PLAY **HOCKEY?**

... A HOCKEY **TICK!**

WHAT HAS **18 LEGS** AND **CATCHES FLIES?**

... A **BASEBALL TEAM!**

HAT IS A **SPACE CRITTER'S** FAVORITE **CANDY BAR?**

... A **MILKY WAY!**

WHEN ARE PEOPLE *UPSIDE DOWN?*

... WHEN THEIR *NOSE RUNS*
AND THEIR *FEET SMELL!*

WHY WAS THE *JIGSAW PUZZLE* UPSET?

... IT WAS GOING TO *PIECES!*

RHYME TIME!

What do you call
a tailor?

A sew pro!

 OW DID THE **BASKETBALL COURT** GET **WET?**

... THE PLAYERS **DRIBBLED** ALL OVER IT!

What do you call
a box
of chocolates?

A sweet treat!

WHAT TYPE OF *FRUIT* WATCHES TOO MUCH *TV?*

... *A COUCH TOMATO!*

NED: WHERE'S YOUR *BROTHER?*
FRED: PLAYING A *DUET.* I FINISHED *FIRST!*

WHAT'S A *WAITER'S* FAVORITE PART OF A *BASKETBALL GAME?*

 ... THE *TIP*-OFF!

Oh, no... it's **The Moe & Joe Show!** ®

HAT KIND OF **COOKIES** SHOULD YOU **EAT** ON A **ROWBOAT?**

... **OAR**-EOS!

HEN IS A **CHINESE RESTAURANT** SUCCESSFUL?

... WHEN IT MAKES A **FORTUNE, COOKIE.**

FRED: WHY ARE YOU GETTING **GLASSES** FOR YOUR PET **PORCUPINE?**
NED: BECAUSE HE THOUGHT MY **CACTUS** WAS HIS **GIRLFRIEND!**

What do you
call a blonde dude?

A yellow fellow!

WHEN IS IT **MOST UNLUCKY** TO HAVE A **BLACK CAT** CROSS YOUR **PATH?**

... WHEN YOU'RE A **MOUSE!**

JACQUE: DOCTOR, I AM VERY **NERVOUS.** THIS IS MY **FIRST OPERATION!**
DOC: I CAN RELATE, IT'S **MY FIRST OPERATION,** TOO!

RHYME TIME!®

What do you call
a Star Wars
soft drink?

A Yoda soda!

Oh, no... it's **The Moe & Joe Show!** ® *Moe*: Say, Joe! What is sawdust?

Joe: Well, Moe... the past tense of see dust!

SKIP: DID **YOU** MEET YOUR **MOTHER** AT THE **AIRPORT?**

FLIP: NO, I'VE KNOWN HER FOR **YEARS!**

MOM: WHY WON'T **YOU** TAKE MELVIN TO THE **ZOO?**

DAD: IF THEY WANT HIM, LET **THEM** COME AND GET **HIM!**

JESS: CAN **YOU** TELL THE **SCORE** OF A **FOOTBALL GAME** BEFORE IT **STARTS?**

BESS: YES, **NOTHING** TO **NOTHING!**

WHAT DO **YOU** GET WHEN YOU CROSS A **MONKEY** WITH **DYNAMITE?**

YOE!

... BA-**BOOMS!**

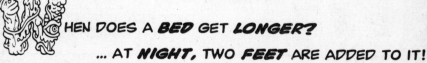

WHEN DOES A **BED** GET **LONGER?**

... AT **NIGHT,** TWO **FEET** ARE ADDED TO IT!

What do you call a hula hoop?

A rad fad!

OW DO COMEDIANS STAY IN **SHAPE?**

... BY DOING **STAND-UPS!**

WHAT DO **YOU** SAY WHEN YOU **STUB** YOUR **TOE** ON THE **SOFA?**

... "C-OUCH!"

WHY WAS THE **DOG'S NOSE** FLAT?

... BECAUSE HE CHASED **PARKED CARS!**

WHAT IS THE **BEST WAY** TO **TALK** TO A **MONSTER?**

 ... **LONG DISTANCE!**

JEAN: STOP PLAYING THAT **GUITAR** OR I'LL GO **NUTS!**
DEAN: TOO LATE, I STOPPED AN **HOUR** AGO!

WHY WAS THE **LAMB** WANDERING AROUND IN THE **MIDDLE** OF THE **NIGHT?**

... BECAUSE SHE WAS **SHEEP**-WALKING!

WHERE DID THE **SLEEPY HIKER** TAKE A **REST** WHEN HE GOT **TIRED?**

... IN HIS **NAP**-SACK

WHAT KIND OF *MARKS* DOES A *KING* LEAVE ON THE *GROUND*?

... FOOT-*PRINCE*!

What do you call a man who's not nice?

A rude dude!

WHAT *ARTIST* LIKES TO DRAW FUNNY-LOOKING *VEHICLES*?

... A *CAR*-TOONIST!

FRED: DID YOU NOTICE HOW MY *VOICE* FILLED THE WHOLE *AUDITORIUM*?
NED: YEAH, LOTS OF *PEOPLE* LEFT TO MAKE *ROOM* FOR IT!

What does a high school student want to be?

A glad grad!

WHERE DID THE *MONSTER* KEEP HIS *EXTRA PAIR* OF *ARMS?*

... IN A *HAND*-BAG!

HY DID THE *WAITER* ALWAYS *WIN* AT *TENNIS?*

... HE HAD THE BEST *SERVE!*

WHAT IS A *YOUNG SNAKE'S* FAVORITE *SCHOOL SUBJECT?*

 ... *HISS*-TORY!

HAT SHOULD **YOU** DO IF YOU FIND A **MONSTER** IN YOUR **BED?**
... **SLEEP SOMEWHERE ELSE!**

WHAT'S **BLACK** AND **YELLOW** AND HAS **CURLY HAIR?**
... A **FRIZZ-BEE!**

What's a good name for an elephant's trunk?

A nose hose!

WHAT DOES A *NEWBORN FARM* WEAR ON ITS *HEAD*?

... A BABY *BARN*-ET!

WHAT DO *YOU* GET WHEN YOU *COMBINE SUPERHEROES* WITH *OVERNIGHT PACKAGES*?

... *FED-X-MEN!*

What do you call a day of shopping? A mall crawl!

WHAT **COUNTRY EATS** THE MOST **FRIED FOOD?**

... **GREECE!**

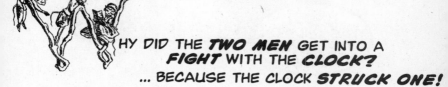

HY DID THE **TWO MEN** GET INTO A **FIGHT** WITH THE **CLOCK?**

... BECAUSE THE CLOCK **STRUCK ONE!**

SUE: WHY DO YOU LOOK SO **EXHAUSTED?**
STU: I WAS **UP ALL NIGHT** STUDYING FOR MY **BLOOD TEST!**

Oh, no... it's **The Moe & Joe Show!** ® *Moe:* Say, Joe! Did you hear the joke about the pencil?

 Joe: Well, Moe... yeah, it was pointless!

WHY CAN'T *YOU* STAND ON YOUR *HEAD?*

... IT'S TOO *HIGH UP!*

What do you call a small person who lives in a bottle?

A teeny genie!

WALTER: *WAITER!* THERE'S A *FLY*
IN MY *SOUP!*
WAITER: WELL, THE *COOK* USED TO BE
A *TAILOR!*

What do you call
a nice perfume?

A swell smell!

CHRISSY: *TEARS* COME TO MY *EYES*
WHEN I *SING!*
MISSY: TRY PUTTING SOME *COTTON*
IN YOUR *EARS!*

JAYNE: DID *YOU* KNOW THAT YOU *BREATHE*
THROUGH THE *PORES* OF YOUR *SKIN?*
LANE: WOW! WHAT'LL THEY *THINK* OF *NEXT!*

 Oh, no... it's **The Moe & Joe Show!** ®   *Moe:* Say, Joe! What is the dumbest state?

 Joe: Well, Moe... Flori-duh!

KAREN: WHY ARE **YOU** WEARING MY **NEW RAINCOAT** WITHOUT **ASKING?**
SHARON: I DIDN'T WANT TO GET YOUR **NEW SWEATER** WET!

MIKE: MY **HAIR** IS GETTING PRETTY **THIN!**
IKE: SO, WHO WANTS **FAT** HAIR?

 Oh, no... it's **The Moe & Joe Show!** ® *Moe*: Say, Joe! What flower is an athlete?

 Joe: Well, Moe... a lily of the volleyball!

WHAT *PET* PLAYS
IN THE *MARCHING BAND?*

... THE TRUM-*PET!*

KRIS: A *GLASS* FELL OVER AND *DIDN'T*
SPILL ONE DROP OF *MILK!*
SIS: IT WAS FULL OF *ORANGE JUICE!*

What do you call
a gross mallard?

A yucky ducky!

CODY: WELL, I'M SORRY *YOU* DON'T LIKE THE *FOOD!* I'VE BEEN *COOKING* SINCE *BEFORE* YOU WERE *BORN!*

JODY: FINE, BUT DID *YOU* HAVE TO CHOOSE *NOW* TO *SERVE* IT?

LAD: DAD, WILL *YOU* GET ME A *SUNDAE?*

DAD: REMIND ME *LATER*, IT'S ONLY *TUESDAY!*

WHAT DO **YOU** CALL A **MONSTER'S SELF ESTEEM**?

... THE **PRIDE** OF FRANKENSTEIN!

JON: MY **TEACHER** YELLED AT ME FOR SOMETHING **I DIDN'T DO**!
DON: WHAT WAS IT?
JON: MY **HOMEWORK**!

Oh, no... it's **The Moe & Joe Show!** ® *Moe:* Say, Joe! My fish got away!

Joe: Well, Moe... it's a herring loss!

WHAT'S A *TURTLE'S* FAVORITE *DRINK?*

... *SNAP*-PLE!

WHY DID THE *FORTUNE TELLER* GET ALL *DRESSED UP?*

... SHE WAS GOING TO THE *CRYSTAL BALL!*

WHAT DO *YOU* GET WHEN YOU CROSS THE *ATLANTIC OCEAN* AND THE *BALTIC SEA?*

... A *BIG* BOAT!

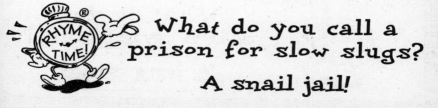

What do you call a prison for slow slugs?

A snail jail!

LUKE: I GOT AN "F" ON MY **TEST** BECAUSE I DIDN'T REMEMBER WHERE THE **EQUATOR** WAS!

DUKE: NEXT TIME REMEMBER WHERE YOU **PUT THINGS!**

What do you call a symphony?

A long song!

MATTY: WHAT ABOUT THE *RACE*
IN THE *KITCHEN?*
PATTY: THE *LETTUCE* CAME OUT *AHEAD,*
THE *WATER* KEPT ON *RUNNING,* AND
THE *TOMATO* TRIED TO *CATCH UP!*

 REBA THE AMOEBA: DID YOU HEAR ABOUT
THE *DUDE* WHO SWAM *HALFWAY*
ACROSS THE *ENGLISH CHANNEL?*
SHEBA THE AMOEBA: HE DECIDED HE
COULDN'T MAKE IT SO HE *SWAM BACK!*

Oh, no... it's **The Moe & Joe Show!** ® **Moe**: Say, Joe! Why do you keep scratching yourself?

Joe: Well, Moe... I'm the one who knows where it itches!

WHAT DID THE *CAT SAY* WHEN SHE *SPILLED* HER *MILK?*

... "NOBODY'S *PURR*-FECT!"

WHY DID THE *BOY* BRING *SCISSORS* TO *SCHOOL?*

... HE WANTED TO *CUT* THE *LUNCH LINE!*

WHAT PART OF YOUR *EYE* GOES TO *SCHOOL?*

... THE *PUPIL!*

CRAIG: CAN YOU *CARRY* A *TUNE?*
GREG: YOU JUST *HEARD* ME *SING!*
CRAIG: WELL, CARRY *THAT* THING OUTSIDE
AND *THROW IT* IN THE *GARBAGE!*

What do you call an energetic chimp?

A spunky monkey!

WHAT KIND OF *FISH* CAN YOU *BUILD* THINGS WITH?

... A *HAMMER*-HEAD SHARK!

WHAT CAUSED THE *DUCK* TO GET *SICK?*

... *BEAK*-TERIA!

WHAT SHOULDN'T *YOU* DRINK WHEN YOU HAVE A *COLD?*

... *COUGH*-EE!

What do you call a school of fish?

A bass class!

WHAT DO *YOU* WRITE WITH WHILE *RIDING* IN AN *AIRPLANE?*

 ... A *HIGH*-LIGHTER!

DID *YOU* HEAR ABOUT THE *MONKEY* THAT *LOOKED* JUST LIKE HIS *FATHER?*

... YEAH, HE WAS A *CHIMP* OFF THE OLD BLOCK!

RHYME TIME!

What do you call a riddle about a frog?

A croak joke!

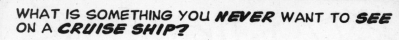

WHAT IS SOMETHING YOU **NEVER** WANT TO **SEE** ON A **CRUISE SHIP?**

... A **SINK!**

WHAT DO **YOU** GET WHEN YOU EAT **TOO MUCH BREAKFAST?**

... **WAF-FULL!**

WHAT COMES FROM ANOTHER **PLANET** AND TASTES GOOD IN **HOT CHOCOLATE?**

... **MARTIAN**-MELLOWS!

Oh, no... it's **The Moe & Joe Show!** ® **Moe:** Say, Joe! What kind of drink does your dad like?

Joe: Well, Moe... Pop-si-cola!

WHAT PART OF YOUR *SHOE* IS MOST LIKE YOUR *MOUTH?*

... THE *TONGUE!*

W HAT *DRINK* ALWAYS NEEDS THINGS *REPEATED?*

... *WHAT*-ER!

WHAT *CARTOON DOG* WOULD MAKE A *GOOD SPY?*

... *SNOOPY!*

RHYME TIME! ®

What do you call a bicycle that doesn't work?

A broke spoke!

WHY WAS THE *COMPUTER* IN THE *FREEZER?*

... BECAUSE IT WAS *FROZEN!*

YOE!

WHAT IS A *SAILOR'S* FAVORITE *DRINK?*
... PEP-*SEA!*

MOM: HOW DID THE *SUN* GET *BROKEN?*
TOM: I DON'T KNOW, BUT IT'S BEEN LIKE THAT
SINCE THE *CRACK* OF *DAWN!*

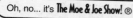 Oh, no... it's **The Moe & Joe Show!** ® *Moe:* Say, Joe! What article of clothing hates summer?

 Joe: Well, Moe... sweat-ers!

OW DO *YOU* KNOW IF A *KITTEN* HAS A *BROKEN LEG?*

... DO A *CAT-SCAN!*

WHAT *PART* OF THE *BODY* CAN BE USED TO WRAP *PRESENTS?*

Yoe!

... THE EL-*BOW!*

What do you call it when teddy bears fall in love?

A plush crush!

WHY DID THE *TOILET* GO TO THE *DOCTOR?*
... IT WAS FEELING *FLUSHED!*

*W*HAT *OFFICE SUPPLY* CAN YOU *PLAY CARDS* WITH?
... THE ROLO-*DECKS!*

Oh, no... it's **The Moe & Joe Show!** ® **Moe**: Say, Joe! What kind of monkey talks a lot?

Joe: Well, Moe... babble-boons!

Oh, no... it's **The Moe & Joe Show!** ®

Moe: Say, Joe! What part of a tulip is most like a lamp?

Joe: Well, Moe... the bulb!

HY DID THE *CASHEW* GO SEE A *PSYCHIATRIST?*

... HE WAS FEELING *NUTTY!*

WHAT KIND OF *FISH* WORKS AT A *HOSPITAL?*

... A *STURGEON!*

WHAT *NATION* DOES *CREATIVITY* COME FROM?

... YOUR *IMAGI*-NATION!

What do you call a group of boring musicians?

A bland band!

WHAT DO **YOU** GET WHEN YOU **CROSS** A **BARBER** AND A **LIBRARIAN?**

... A **BARBARIAN!**

WHAT DO **YOU** CALL A **MOUSE** THAT JUST TOOK A **SHOWER?**

... **SQUEAK**-Y CLEAN!

WHY DID THE *JOGGER* GO TO THE *DOCTOR?*

... HE WAS FEELING *RUN* DOWN!

HOW DO *YOU* SPELL *COLORADO?*

THE *RIVER* OR THE *STATE?*

WHAT DOES A *BABY CORN KERNEL* CALL ITS *FATHER?*

... *POPCORN!*

RHYME TIME!

What do you call a pig that's not very cool?

A dorky porky!

WHY DID THE *GHOUL* WANT TO LEAVE *SUMMER CAMP?*

... BECAUSE HE MISSED HIS *MUMMY!*

Oh, no... it's **The Moe & Joe Show!** ® *Moe*: Say, Joe! What has legs but can't walk?

 Joe: Well, Moe... a table!

What do you call
a bunch of flowers
that aren't so pretty?

An okay bouquet!

WHAT DO *YOU* CALL A *CRAB* THAT GIVES
PRESENTS TO *GOOD BOYS* AND *GIRLS?*

... *SANDY CLAWS!*

What do you call
a rhino surrounded
by lions?

A grey prey!

...A COMB!

HAT KIND OF **POOL** HAS **NO WATER?**

... A **CARPOOL!**

WHAT DO **YOU** CALL AN **ENGLISHMAN** WHO EATS **50 SANDWICHES** A **DAY?**

... SIR **LUNCH-A-LOT!**

Oh, no... it's **The Moe & Joe Show!** ® *Moe:* Say, Joe! What has an eye but can't see?

 Joe: Well, Moe... a needle!

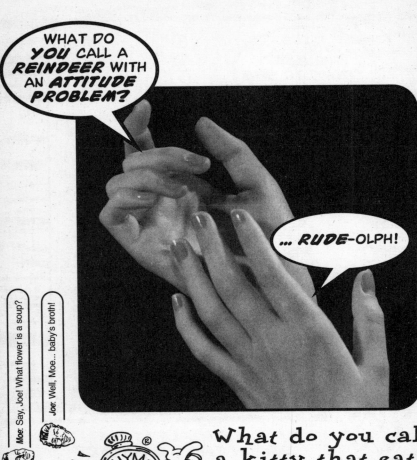

RHYME TIME! ®

What do you call a kitty that eats too much?

A fat cat!

WHY SHOULDN'T **YOU** TELL A **PIG** YOUR **SECRETS?**

... BECAUSE HE'LL **SQUEAL!**

WHAT DO **ESKIMOS** EAT FOR **BREAKFAST** DURING THE **WINTER?**

 ... **ICE CREAM** OF **WHEAT!**

WHY DIDN'T THE **BASKETBALL TEAM** LIKE THEIR **TEAM PHOTO?**

... IT WAS A **FOUL** SHOT!

WHAT DO **YOU** CALL A **GROUP** OF **BEES** THAT ARE ALWAYS **FIGHTING?**

... **RUMBLE** BEES!

WHY IS THE LETTER "**A**" LIKE A **FLOWER?**

... BECAUSE A "**B**" COMES AFTER IT!

What do you call a tool that's placed on a chair?

A bench wrench!

WHY DID THE **COW** GET A **SECOND JOB?**

... BECAUSE HE NEEDED TO MAKE MORE **MOO-LAH!**

HAT DO **VIRUSES** LIKE TO **EAT?**

... CHICKEN **POX**-PIE!

 Oh, no... it's **The Moe & Joe Show!** ® **Moe**: Say, Joe! What is a runner's favorite part of a car?

 Joe: Well, Moe... the dash-board!

WHAT DID THE **MOMMY MONSTER** SAY TO HER **SON**
... "QUIT PICKING YOUR **NOSES!**"

HOW DID THE **INVISIBLE MAN'S MOTHER** KNOW HE WAS **LYING?**

... SHE COULD **SEE** RIGHT **THROUGH** HIM

Oh, no... it's **The Moe & Joe Show!** ® *Moe*: Say, Joe! What is a frog's favorite soft drink?

Joe: Well, Moe... Croak-a-Cola!

WHY DID THE **VAMPIRE** GO TO THE **DOCTOR?**

... BECAUSE HE WAS **COFFIN!**

WHY DID THE **SLACKER** GET A JOB IN A **BAKERY?**

... HE LIKED TO **LOAF** AROUND!

WHAT DO **YOU** TAKE TO GET TO THE **ROOF** OF YOUR **MOUTH?**

... THE **SALI**-VATOR!

What do you call a bag that carries ballots?

A vote tote!

Oh, no... it's **The Moe & Joe Show!** ® **Moe:** Say, Joe! What part of a duck is most like a spider?

Joe: Well, Moe... its web-bed feet!

HY WAS THE **JELLYFISH** AFRAID OF **EVERYTHING?**

... BECAUSE IT WAS **SPINELESS!**

WHERE DO **GLASSES** LIKE TO GO ON **SATURDAY NIGHTS?**

... TO THE **EYE-BALL!**

What do you call a celebrity's limo?

A star car!

WHAT DO ***YOU*** CALL AN ***INJURED TYRANNOSAURUS REX?***

... A DINO-***SORE!***

WHAT DID THE ***BUTCHER*** SAY TO THE ***BOLOGNA?***

... "NICE TO ***MEAT*** YOU!"

HOW DID THE ***COOK*** INVENT ***MACARONI?***

... HE USED HIS ***NOODLE!***

ROSE: DID **YOU** HEAR ABOUT THE **CARTOON CHARACTER** WHO HAD AN **UPSET STOMACH?**

LILY: HIS NAME WAS **BARF** SIMPSON!

WHY DO **YOU** NEED **GLASSES** WHEN SPELLING **MISSISSIPPI?**

... YOU NEED **FOUR I'S!**

JOY: DID **YOU** HEAR ABOUT THE **CARTOON CHARACTER** WHO HAD **GAS?**

ROY: HIS NAME WAS **FART** SIMPSON!

HAT **SPORT** DOES THE **EASTER BUNNY** LIKE TO **PLAY?**

... **BASKET**-BALL

What do you call a really good Christmas?

A cool yule!

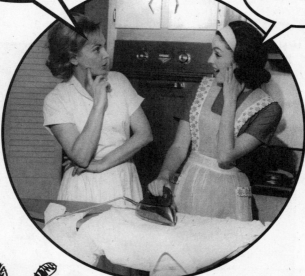

WHAT **SPORT** DO **YELLOWJACKETS** LIKE TO **PLAY?**

... FRIS-**BEE!**

HAT DO **YOU** CALL THE **KING** OF THE **JUNGLE** WHEN HE'S **CRYING?**

... **TEAR**-ZAN!

WHAT IS AN **ARCHITECT'S** FAVORITE **HOBBY?**

... BODY-**BUILDING!**

Oh, no... it's **The Moe & Joe Show!** ® *Moe*: Say, Joe! What breakfast cereal is used to protect castles?

Joe: Well, Moe... moat-meal!

Oh, no... it's **The Moe & Joe Show!** ® **Moe**: Say, Joe! How do fish communicate with each other?

 Joe: Well, Moe... they use sea-mail!

WHICH **TREE** IS ALWAYS **EMBARRASSED?**

...A **RED OAK!**

LIZIA ONE: DID **YOU** HEAR ABOUT THE **WAITER** WHO COULD **FLY?**

LIZIA TWO: YEAH, HE WAS A REAL **SUPPER** HERO!

WHAT DID THE **GHOST** GIVE HIS **GIRLFRIEND** FOR HER **BIRTHDAY?**

... A **BOO**-QUET OF FLOWERS!

CHIP: DID *YOU* HEAR ABOUT THE *ABSENTMINDED LION TAMER?*

CHOP: HE KEPT FORGETTING HIS *LIONS!*

BURT: WHY DOES MY *PET SPIDER* LIKE TO USE MY *COMPUTER* SO MUCH?

KURT: IT LIKES TO CHECK OUT *WEB SITES!*

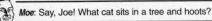

Oh, no... it's **The Moe & Joe Show!** ® *Moe:* Say, Joe! What cat sits in a tree and hoots?

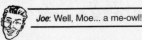

Joe: Well, Moe... a me-owl!

WHO IS THE **SKINNIEST BOY** IN SCHOOL?

... NA-**THIN!**

What do you call a group of detectives?

A clue crew!

WHY WAS THE **SHOE** SHY?

... IT WAS **TONGUE-TIED!**

WHY WAS THE *MOON* FULL?

... BECAUSE IT *ATE* TOO MUCH

WHAT *COWBOY* WORE A LOT OF *PERFUME?*

... THE *COLOGNE* RANGER!

WHAT'S A GOOD *INSTRUMENT* TO GIVE SOMEONE WHO DOESN'T HAVE A *MUSICAL BONE* IN THEIR *BODY?*

... A TROM-*BONE!*

WHAT KIND OF *SOUP* DOES *MICKEY MOUSE'S GIRLFRIEND* LIKE?

... *MINNIE*-STRONE!

What do you call a bad cut from the barber?

A hair scare!

What do you call an adorable peach?
A cute fruit!

WHAT KIND OF *GUM* DOES A WHALE *CHEW?*

... *BLUBBER* GUM!

WHAT DO *YOU* GIVE A *MARE* WHO'S ABOUT TO GET *MARRIED?*

... A *BRIDLE* PARTY!

Oh, no... it's **The Moe & Joe Show!** ® *Moe*: Say, Joe! What is a tailor's favorite drink?

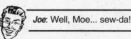 *Joe*: Well, Moe... sew-da!

WHAT DOES A *SQUIRREL* WITH A *SORE TOOTH* EAT?

... *ACHE*-CORNS!

HY DID THE *SHEEP* GO TO THE *DOCTOR?*

... BECAUSE IT WAS FEELING *BAA-D!*

WHERE DO *COWS* POST THEIR *MESSAGES* AT *WORK?*

... ON THE *BULL*-ETIN BOARD!

Oh, no... it's **The Moe & Joe Show!** ® **Moe**: Say, Joe! What girl always copies pictures?

 Joe: Well, Moe... Trace-y!

WHAT IS A *WORM'S* FAVORITE *CITY?*

... THE BIG *APPLE!*

HAT *ANIMALS* ARE THE BEST *SWIMMERS?*

... *ELEPHANTS*--THEY ALWAYS
HAVE THEIR *TRUNKS* ON

What do you call
a fat frog?

A bog hog!

WHAT DOES A *SNEEZE* USE TO *JUMP* OUT OF A *PLANE?*

... A PAR-*AH-CHOO*-TE!

WHAT PART OF YOUR *HOUSE* IS MOST LIKE AN *ANIMAL?*

... THE *SEAL*-ING!

WHAT DO *PEOPLE* WHO WORK ON *WALL STREET* LOVE MOST ABOUT *CHRISTMAS?*

... THE *STOCK*-INGS!

WHAT HAPPENS WHEN **YOU** LEAVE **KRUSTY THE CLOWN** OUT IN THE **RAIN?**

... HE BECOMES **RUSTY** THE CLOWN!

HERE DO **COWS** AND **CHICKENS** GO TO GET **MEDICINE?**

... THE **FARM**-ACIST!

Oh, no... it's **The Moe & Joe Show!** ®   *Moe*: Say, Joe! Why are monkeys the best storytellers?

Joe: Well, Moe... they have long tales!

my country 'tis of HEE DEPARTMENT

WHAT STATE HAS THE MOST *BILLS?*

... I-*OWE*-A!

WHAT STATE *BREATHES* THE MOST?

... *AIR*-IZONA!

WHAT STATE CAN YOU *BAKE* WITH?

... *FLOUR*-IDA!

WHAT STATE DO YOU GO TO WHEN YOU GET SENT TO *PRISON?*

... *CON*-NECTICUT!

WHAT STATE HAS THE MOST *ACORNS?*

... *OAK*-LAHOMA!

WHAT STATE TALKS ON THE *PHONE* THE MOST?

... *CALL*-ORADO!

WHAT STATE IS IN THE MIDDLE OF YOUR *LEG*?

... *KNEE*-BRASKA!

WHAT'S A *PIG'S* FAVORITE STATE?

... NEW-*PORK!*

WHAT IS THE MOST *INQUISITIVE* STATE?

... *WHY*-OMING!

WHAT IS A *WRITER'S* FAVORITE STATE?

... *PEN*-SYLVANIA!

WHAT STATE LOOKS MOST LIKE YOUR *BEDROOM*?

... *MESS*-ACHUSETTS!

WHAT *STATE* HAS THE MOST *DIRTY LAUNDRY*?

... NEW *HAMPER*-SHIRE!

WHAT IS A *COMEDIAN'S* FAVORITE STATE?

... UT-*HA!*

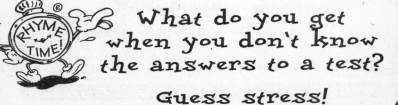

WHAT DO *YOU* GET WHEN YOU CROSS A
YELLOW CANARY
WITH A *MUPPET?*

... *TWEETY BERT!*

YOE!

WHAT DO *YOU* CALL A *DOCTOR'S*
ASSISTANT WITH *NO MONEY?*

... A *POOR*-A-MEDIC!

Oh, no... it's **The Moe & Joe Show!** ®   **Moe**: Say, Joe! Why don't you want to go on the airplane?

 Joe: Well, Moe... it's too flight-ening!

WHAT **SIGN** DOES A **MONSTER** PUT UP WHEN
HE GOES ON **VACATION** TO A **LAKE?**

... **"GOON** FISHIN'!"

What do you call the
stairs that lead to a
chicken's house?

A coop stoop!

 HO LOOKS LIKE *KRUSTY THE CLOWN* BUT *ISN'T?*

... KRUSTY THE *CLONE!*

WHAT HAPPENED WHEN THE *DOCTOR* TOLD A *JOKE* DURING *SURGERY?*

 ... THE PATIENT WAS LEFT *IN STITCHES!*

Oh, no... it's **The Moe & Joe Show!** ® **Moe**: Say, Joe! What do gnomes eat when they're hungry?

Joe: Well, Moe... micro-chips!

WHAT KIND OF *SOUP* DOES A *DOG* LIKE?

... CHICKEN *POODLE!*

WHY COULDN'T THE *DRAGON* HOLD HIS *JOB?*

... HE KEPT GETTING *FIRED!*

WHAT *VEGETABLE* DID THE *PILGRIM* GET *LOST* IN?

... MAIZE

What's a hip queen called?

A cooler ruler!

I THINK YOU *CHEATED* WHEN YOU *PASSED OUT* THE *CARDS!*

... *DEAL* WITH IT!

IF *YOU SPEND* ALL OF YOUR *MONEY* ON *PERFUME,* YOU'LL HAVE *SCENTS* BUT NO *DOLLARS!*

 WHERE DOES A **SQUIRREL** WRITE HIS **CLASS ASSIGNMENT?**

... IN A **NUT**-BOOK!

WHAT IS **ORANGE** AND GOES "**SLAM, SLAM, SLAM, SLAM**"?

Yoe!

... A FOUR-DOOR **CARROT!**

WHAT DO **YOU** CALL IT WHEN A **SNAKE** THROWS A **TANTRUM?**

... A **HISS**-Y FIT!

RHYME TIME!®

What do you call a lawyer who looks like a bird?

A legal eagle!

 HAT'S *BIG, GREEN,* LIVES IN *NEW YORK,* AND HAS A *COLD?*

... THE ST-*AH-CHOO* OF LIBERTY!

What do you get
when you eat
sweets on the beach?

Sandy candy!

WHAT DOES THE *SUN* PUT
ON *GIFT PACKAGES?*

... A RAIN-*BOW!*

WHAT IS THE *RESULT* WHEN ONE
STRAWBERRY MEETS
ANOTHER *STRAWBERRY?*

... A STRAWBERRY *SHAKE!*

What happens when a bird bumps into something?

A wing ding!

WHAT IS A *HAWAIIAN'S* FAVORITE *CAR?*

... CHEVRO-*LEI*

WHAT DID THE *CEREAL* SAY TO THE *DOG?*

... "SNAP! CRACKLE! *PUP!*"

WHAT DO THEY CALL THE *GHOST* THAT SINGS LIKE *FRANK SINATRA?*

... OLD *BOO* EYES!

Oh, no... it's **The Moe & Joe Show!** ® **Moe:** Say, Joe! What animal takes care of kids?

 Joe: Well, Moe... a nanny goat!

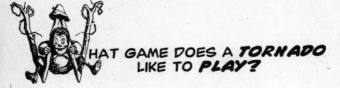

WHAT GAME DOES A *TORNADO* LIKE TO *PLAY?*

... *TWISTER*

WHAT IS *WRAPPING PAPER'S* FAVORITE *SPORT?*

... *BOW*-LING!

WHY DID THE *POSTMAN* GO HOME *EARLY?*

... HE *HEARD* THERE WAS GOING TO BE A *STAMP*-EDE!

Oh, no... it's **The Moe & Joe Show!** ® *Moe*: Say, Joe! What is a termite's favorite drink?

 Joe: Well, Moe... rot beer!

HY COULDN'T THE *MOTORCYCLE* PASS THE *18-WHEELER*?

... IT WAS *TWO TIRED!*

WHAT IS *CASPER'S* FAVORITE *MEAL*?

... *SPOOK*-GHETTI!

What do you call a lecture by an ocean?

A beach speech!

WHAT IS A *DOG'S* FAVORITE *BASEBALL* POSITION?

... *POOCH*-ER!

What do you call an animated monster?

A toon goon!

Oh, no... it's **The Moe & Joe Show!** ® *Moe*: Say, Joe! What kind of motorcycle does a bull ride?

Joe: Well, Moe... a Cow-asaki!

WHAT DO *YOU* GET WHEN YOU CROSS *CAMPBELL'S* WITH *CLARK KENT?*

... *SOUP*-ER MAN!

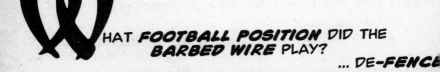

WHAT IS THE *SMELLIEST CABLE CHANNEL?*
... H-*B-O!*

WHAT *FOOTBALL POSITION* DID THE *BARBED WIRE* PLAY?
... DE-*FENCE*

What do you call an activity that isn't much fun?

A lame game!

WHAT **CANDY BAR** DOES A **COMEDIAN** LIKE?

WHAT **CANDY** DO YOU EAT IN THE **SCHOOLYARD?**

... **RECESS** PIECES!

WHAT DO **YOU** GET WHEN YOU CROSS **SNOOPY** WITH A **HORNET?**

... A **BEE**-GLE!

WHAT IS AN **ASTRONAUT'S** FAVORITE **CAR?**

... A MUS-**TANG!**

Oh, no... it's **The Moe & Joe Show!** ®

 Moe: Say, Joe! What position does the elevator play?

 Joe: Well, Moe... lift field!

What do you call a joke about Attila?

A hun pun!

WHAT DO *MOTORCYCLISTS* WATCH ON *TV?*

... THE *LEATHER* CHANNEL!

WHAT *POSITION* DOES THE *DRY CLEANER* PLAY?

... *SHIRT* STOP!

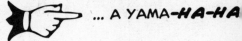

WHAT KIND OF *MOTORCYCLE* DOES A *RIDDLE WRITER* DRIVE?

... A YAMA-*HA-HA*

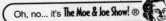 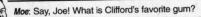

Oh, no... it's **The Moe & Joe Show!** ®   *Moe:* Say, Joe! What is Clifford's favorite gum?

Joe: Well, Moe... Big Red!

What do you call a smelly animal with a mohawk?

A punk skunk!

WHAT IS A *JUDGE'S* FAVORITE *CAR?*

... AN ES-*COURT!*

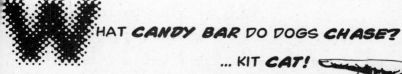

WHAT IS A *LUMBERJACK'S* FAVORITE *FRUIT?*

... *PINE*-APPLE!

WHAT *CANDY BAR* DO DOGS *CHASE?*

... KIT *CAT!*

Oh, no... it's **The Moe & Joe Show!** ®   *Moe*: Say, Joe! What do vampires eat at a baseball game?

Joe: Well, Moe... fang-furters!

HOW DOES *SHAMU* TRAVEL *CROSS-COUNTRY*?

... THE *WHALE* ROAD!

OW DOES A *FIRE-EATER* LIKE HIS *STEAKS*?

... *FLAME* BROILED

What do you call a roll that's finished baking?

A done bun!

 WHAT IS A **CANARY'S** FAVORITE **CEREAL?**

... SHREDDED **TWEET!**

LOU: DID **YOU** HEAR ABOUT THE **GRANDMOTHER** WHO WON **FIRST PRIZE?**

SUE: IT WAS ON THE **GRANNY AWARDS!**

HAT DOES **WOODY WOODPECKER** LIKE TO DO IN A **PARK?**

... GO ON A **PECK**-NIC!

 OW DID THE **BODYBUILDER** KNOCK OVER THE **DENTIST?** ... HE HAD **STRONG BREATH!**

WHY ARE **CALCULATORS** SO **RELIABLE?**
... BECAUSE YOU CAN **COUNT** ON THEM!

What do you call someone who's obsessed with mummies?

A Tut nut!

HAT IS A *WIZARD'S* BEST SCHOOL *SUBJECT?*

 ... *SPELL*-ING!

 HY DID THE **WATCH** GET INTO **TROUBLE** AT **SCHOOL?**

... IT WAS ALL **WOUND** UP!

WHAT DOES **SANTA** USE TO MOW THE **LAWN?**

... A **SNOWPLOWER!**

RHYME TIME!

What do you call someone who knows a lot about paintings?

Art smart!

WHAT DO *YOU* GET WHEN YOU CROSS A *LIFT* WITH *LUKE SKYWALKER'S DAD?*

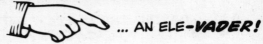 ... AN ELE-*VADER!*

WHY DID THE *COP* STOP THE *COMET?*

... SHE WAS TRAVELING OVER THE *SPEED OF LIGHT LIMIT!*

WHAT IS A *CHICKEN'S* FAVORITE *CAR?*

... AN *EGGS*-PLORER!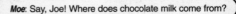

Oh, no... it's **The Moe & Joe Show!** ® *Moe*: Say, Joe! Where does chocolate milk come from?

Joe: Well, Moe... brown cows!

Where do you
buy gruesome
Halloween costumes?

A gore store!

WHAT DO **YOU** GET WHEN YOU COMBINE
TARDINESS AND **CANDY?**

... CHOCO-**LATE!**

What do you call a colored contact lens?

An eye dye!

WHAT DID THE *SHOE* SAY TO THE *GUM?*

... "DON'T LET PEOPLE WALK *ALL OVER YOU!*"

WHAT IS THE *SPOOKIEST LAKE* IN *AMERICA?*

... LAKE *EERIE!*

WHAT DID THE *BUTTER* SAY WHEN *EVERYTHING* WAS *GOING RIGHT?*

 ... "I'M *ON A ROLL!*"

Oh, no... it's **The Moe & Joe Show!** ® **Moe**: Say, Joe! What is a vampire's favorite holiday?

Joe: Well, Moe... Fangs-giving!

MANNY: DID *YOU* HEAR THE *NATIONAL BIRD*
OF THE *UNITED STATES*
WENT TO *JAIL?*
FANNY: YEAH, HE'S ILL-*EAGLE!*

HY DID THE *GIANT* GET INTO *TROUBLE*
AT *SCHOOL?*

... BECAUSE HE WAS TELLING *TALL TALES*

W HAT DID THE *PAINTING* SAY AFTER
BEING *ARRESTED?*

... I'VE BEEN *FRAMED*

WHAT'S *WHITE,* MADE OF *PORCELAIN,* AND
FOUND IN A *PLAY ROOM?*

... A *TOY*-LET!

Oh, no... it's **The Moe & Joe Show!** ®   *Moe:* Say, Joe! What is the librarian's favorite city?

 Joe: Well, Moe... Reading, PA!

WHAT IS A *LIBRARIAN'S* FAVORITE *CAR?*

... A POR-*SHHHH!*

Oh, no... it's **The Moe & Joe Show!** ® *Moe:* Say, Joe! Why was the pillar sent to jail?

 Joe: Well, Moe... for holding up a house!

WHAT'S THE **BEST ADVICE** YOU CAN GIVE TO **PEANUT BUTTER?**

 ... "STICK TO YOUR **GUMS!**"

What do you use
to fix a flat
on a truck?

A mack jack!

 HAT IS AN *INSECT'S* FAVORITE *SPORT?*

... *BEE*-SKETBALL!

WHAT DID THE *VEGETABLE* SAY TO HER *SON* WHILE IN THE *LIBRARY?*

 ... "*PEAS* WHISPER!"

WHAT DOES A *HEAD* OF *HAIR* EAT FOR *BREAKFAST?*

... *DANDRUFF* FLAKES!

Oh, no... it's **The Moe & Joe Show!** ® *Moe*: Say, Joe! What does a rap star listen to in the car?

 Joe: Well, Moe... the radi-yo!

What do you call a day off from school?
A play day!

WHY DID THE **HAIR** GET **ANGRY** AT THE **HAIRDRESSER?**

... BECAUSE IT WAS TIRED OF BEING **TEASED!**

WHAT DID THE *LAUNDROMAT OWNER* HATE ABOUT THE *BEACH?*

... WAITING FOR THE *TIDE* TO COME IN!

WHAT WAS THE *SNEAKER SALESMAN'S MOTTO?*

... "THERE'S NO BUSINESS LIKE *SHOE BUSINESS!*"

WHAT DID THE *ROBBER* SAY TO THE *POST-IT-NOTE?*

... "STICK 'EM UP!"

HAT IS A *FISHERMAN'S* FAVORITE
BASEBALL POSITION?

... *CATCH*-ER

 WHAT *CANDY BAR* DOES A
MIRROR HATE?

... *CRACKLE*

RHYME TIME!

What do you call Ernie's friend with broken arm?

A hurt Bert!

WHAT IS A *CANNIBAL'S* FAVORITE *CANDY?*

... BUTTER-*FINGERS!*

WHAT IS A *SNOWMAN'S* FAVORITE *BASEBALL POSITION?*

... *FROST* BASE!

Oh, no... it's **The Moe & Joe Show!** ® *Moe*: Say, Joe! What cereal do cows eat?

 Joe: Well, Moe... Fruity Peb-bulls!

MATT: IF YOU WANT TO SPREAD **GOSSIP,** WHAT SHOULD YOU **DO?**

PAT: **TELL**-A-**PHONE!**

WHAT DO **YOU** WEAR ON THE **4TH** OF **JULY?**

... **INDEPEND-PANTS!**

WHAT DID THE **BEE** SAY WHEN IT RETURNED TO THE **HIVE?**

... **"HONEY**, I'M **HOME!"**

WHAT DO **YOU** CALL AN **UNEXCITING PIG?**

YOE!

... A **BOAR!**

HAT DO **YOU** GET WHEN YOU CROSS A **TUG BOAT** WITH **HOMER'S WIFE?**

... **BARGE** SIMPSON!

RHYME TIME!®

What do you get when you eat pasta while napping? Beddy spaghetti!

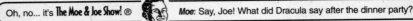

Oh, no... it's **The Moe & Joe Show!** ® *Moe*: Say, Joe! What did Dracula say after the dinner party?

Joe: Well, Moe... "Fang you very much!"

WHAT HAPPENS WHEN YOU *PHONE* A *BEE?*

... YOU GET A *BUZZ*-Y SIGNAL!

WHAT DO *RICH* PEOPLE *EAT* ON THEIR *BIRTHDAY?*

... *24-CARROT* CAKE

RHYME TIME! ®

What do you call someone who rips up their mail?

A letter shredder!

**HAT LETTER IS THE *OPPOSITE* OF *OUT?***

... *N!*

WHAT IS A *GHOST'S* FAVORITE *SPORT?*

... *BOO*-SKETBALL!

WHAT DID THE *GOOSE* SAY WHEN IT WAS *STUCK* IN *TRAFFIC?*

... *"HONK! HONK!"*

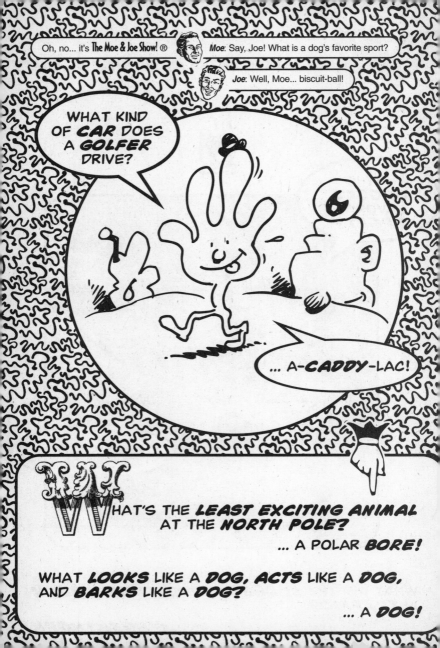

WHAT IS A **BELLY BUTTON'S** FAVORITE **CAR?**

... AN **AUDI!**

...HAT IS AN **OPTOMETRIST'S** FAVORITE **DRINK?**

... DR. **PEEPER!**

HARRISON: WHY IS EVERYBODY **CRYING?**
GARRISON: IT'S **WEEP** YEAR!

What has a beard and helps Cinderella?

A hairy fairy!

Sleeping Beau-tee-hee

DEPARTMENT

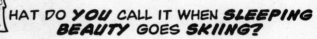

WHAT DO *YOU* CALL IT WHEN *SLEEPING BEAUTY* GOES *SKIING?*

... *SLOPING* BEAUTY!

WHAT DO *YOU* CALL IT WHEN *SLEEPING BEAUTY* FEEDS THE *PIGS?*

... *SLOPPING* BEAUTY!

WHAT DO *YOU* CALL IT WHEN *SLEEPING BEAUTY* STOPS THE *PRINCE* FROM *GETTING FRESH?*

 ... *SLAPPING* BEAUTY!

WHAT DO *YOU* CALL IT WHEN *SLEEPING BEAUTY* FALLS ON THE *ICE?*

... *SLIPPING* BEAUTY!

WHY DID THE **COMPUTER** HATE GOING TO **WORK** EVERY **MORNING?**

... HE HAD A **HARD DRIVE!**

WHAT KIND OF **BUGS** LOVE THE **SNOW?**

... MO-**SKI**-TOS!

What happens when a millionaire gets a rash?

Rich itch!

WHAT DO *YOU* CALL *POPCORN KERNELS* THAT DON'T *POP?*

... *FLOP*-CORN!

WHAT DO **YOU** CALL A **REALLY
JUICY WATERMELON?**

 ... A **WETTER**-MELON!

BEN: THAT SURE IS AN **ANGRY** LOOKING **TREE!**
JEN: DON'T WORRY, ITS **BARK** IS WORSE THAN
ITS **BITE!**

WHY DO **YOU** KEEP **HITTING** YOURSELF IN THE **HEAD** WITH THAT **BASEBALL BAT?**

... BECAUSE YOU TOLD ME I'D HAVE **GOOD LUCK** IF I **KNOCKED** ON **WOOD!**

 What do you call a
sewing box?

A thread shed!

RHYME TIME!

What do you call a taxi that's old and worn out?

A drab cab!

WHAT WAS *FROSTY THE SNOWMAN'S* FAVORITE YEAR AT *SCHOOL?*

... *FROST* GRADE!

BRAD: IS BEING A *PAINTER* VERY *DEMANDING?*
TAD: NO. IT'S *EASEL!*

What do you call
someone who has
crumbs in their hair?

A bread head!

MARK: I THINK OUR **CAT** IS A **GENIUS!**
LARK: WHY?
MARK: BECAUSE I ASKED HER WHAT
ONE MINUS ONE EQUALS
AND SHE SAID **NOTHING!**

HAT DO **YOU** CALL A **GHOST** THAT GOES
TO **COLLEGE?**

... A SCHOOL **SPIRIT!**

WHAT DO **YOU** GET IF YOU COMBINE A **SCOTTISH LEGEND** WITH YOUR **DAD'S WIFE?**

 ... THE LOCH NESS **MOM**-STER!

WHAT DO **YOU** GET IF YOU CROSS **GODZILLA** WITH A **BOTTLE** OF **PERFUME?**

... I DON'T KNOW, BUT I'M NOT GOING TO **SMELL** IT!

Oh, no... it's **The Moe & Joe Show!** ® **Moe:** Say, Joe! What do you call a bald man with a sunburn?

 Joe: Well, Moe... a baked bean!

WHAT IS A *PLUMBER'S* FAVORITE *FRUIT?*

... *WATER*-MELON!

HAT *STATE* IS *OUT OF HERE?*

... ORE-*GONE!*

**HY DID THE *GHOST* GET INTO *TROUBLE* AT THE *DINNER TABLE?***

... HE WAS *GOBLIN* UP HIS FOOD!

WHAT *INSTRUMENT* DOES A *DOCTOR* PLAY?

... THE *FLU*-TE!

WHY DID THE *SHRUB* TAKE A *NAP?*
... BECAUSE HE WAS *BUSHED!*

WHAT IS A *TRAIN'S* FAVORITE *STATE?*

... MASSA-*CHOO-CHOO*-SETTS!

HAT KIND OF *PANTS* ARE THE MOST *ATHLETIC?*

... *PEDAL* PUSHERS!

What do you call an insect that always gets in trouble with the law?

A thug bug!

DAWN: WHAT DO *YOU* CALL A *CAT* THAT'S IN *LOVE*?
FAWN: A *SMITTEN* KITTEN!

WHAT DO *YOU* GET WHEN YOU CROSS A *WINDSTORM* WITH A *VEGETABLE*?

... ASPARA-*GUST!*

Oh, no... it's **The Moe & Joe Show!** ® *Moe*: Say, Joe! What kind of jeans ring?

 Joe: Well, Moe... bell bottoms!

TICKLE A *MULE*... YOU'LL GET A BIG *KICK* OUT OF IT!

TAD: WHY IS YOUR NAME *DAD?*
DAD: BECAUSE I WAS NAMED AFTER MY *FATHER!*

Oh, no... it's **The Moe & Joe Show!** ® *Moe*: Say, Joe! Are the windshield wipers working?

 Joe: Well, Moe... yes, no, yes, no, yes, no, yes, no...!

WHAT DO *YOU* CALL IT WHEN A *BEAN* GOES *SWIMMING?*

... A BEAN *DIP!*

WHAT DO *YOU* CALL A *GROUP* OF *GIRAFFES* GOING TO A *WATERING HOLE?*

... *NECKS* IN LINE!

RHYME TIME! ®

What do you call
a matinee stage
performance?

A day play!

PATIENT: DOCTOR, MY HEAD FEELS FUNNY!
DOCTOR: SO DON'T TOUCH IT!

WHICH POSITION DOES DRACULA PLAY ON THE HOCKEY TEAM?
... GHOULIE!

WHAT IS A BATHTUB'S FAVORITE DESSERT?
... A CAKE OF SOAP!

Oh, no... it's **The Moe & Joe Show!** ® *Moe*: Say, Joe! What bird works in construction?

 Joe: Well, Moe... a crane!

 Oh, no... it's **The Moe & Joe Show!** ® *Moe*: Say, Joe! Why are statues lonely?

 Joe: Well, Moe... people take them for granite!

WHY DID THE **FROG** STUDY ALL **NIGHT?**

... HE WAS **SWAMPED** WITH HOMEWORK!

WHAT DO **YOU** GET WHEN YOU CROSS **LASSIE** WITH A **TULIP?**

JOE!

... **COLLIE FLOWER!**

WHAT DO **YOU** TELL **FROSTY THE SNOWMAN** WHEN HE GETS **UPTIGHT?**

... **"CHILL** OUT!

VICKI: HOW CAN **YOU** TELL IF THERE'S AN **ELEPHANT** IN A **PEANUT BUTTER JAR?**

NICKI: YOU **CAN'T** GET THE **LID** ON!

Oh, no... it's The Moe & Joe Show! ® *Moe*: Say, Joe! What girl makes the best lawyer?

Well, Moe... Law-ra!

WHAT **ITEM** OF **CLOTHING** ALWAYS GETS A GOOD **REPORT CARD?**

... **SMARTY** PANTS!

WHERE DOES **T-REX** GO ON **VACATION?**

... TO THE DINO-**SHORE!**

WHAT DOES A **CHICKEN'S COMPUTER SCREEN** SAY?

... "**CLUCK** HERE!"

What do you call a bagpiper's ugly kilt?

A bad plaid!

THE NAME GAME!

DEPARTMENT

WHAT *GIRL* HAS A LOT OF *SPARE CHANGE?*

... *PENNY!*

WHAT *BOY* IS THE MOST *ADVENTUROUS?*

... *DARE-IN!*

HAT *GIRL* GROWS IN A *GARDEN?*

... *IVY!*

WHAT *BAD GIRL* GROWS IN A *GARDEN?*

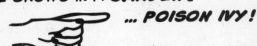 ... *POISON IVY!*

WHAT *BOY* IS THE BEST *PAINTER?*

... *ART*-IE!

**HAT GIRL STYLES HER HAIR THE MOST?**

... AN-*GEL*-A!

WHAT *GIRL* ALWAYS CATCHES THE MOST *FISH?*

... A-*NET*-TE!

 WHAT *BOY* LOVES *CATS?*

... BARTHOLO-*MEOW!*

WHAT *BOY* MAKES THE MOST *MONEY?*

... *EARN*-IE!

HAT *BOY* IS REALLY *DULL?*

... *BORE*-IS!

HAT *BOY* GROWS IN A *GARDEN?*

... *BUD!*

WHAT *GIRL* MAKES THE BEST *CHEERLEADER?*

... DEBO-*RAH RAH!*

HAT *BOY* HAS PET *SHEEP?*

... D-*EWE*-Y!

WHAT *BOY* LOVES *PICKLES?*

... *DILL*-ON!

WHAT DO *YOU* GET WHEN YOU CROSS *KING KONG* WITH *FLEAS?*

... *NERVOUS DOGS*

WHAT KIND OF *GUM* DOES A *BEAR* CHEW?
... *DEN*-TYNE!

BETH: I HEARD *GEORGE JETSON* HAS *GAINED* A LOT OF *WEIGHT!*
SETH: HE'S NOW A *JUMBO JET*-SON!

Oh, no... it's **The Moe & Joe Show!** ® **Moe**: Say, Joe! I love your nose!

Joe: Well, Moe... it runs in my family!

What do you call a puppy that's no longer lost?

A found hound!

Oh, no... it's **The Moe & Joe Show!** ® *Moe*: Say, Joe! What's big and hairy and bounces?

Joe: Well, Moe... King Kong on a trampoline!

WHAT DO *YOU* CALL IT WHEN YOU *WATCH* THE *WIZARD* OF *OZ?*

... A *WITCH WATCH!*

WHAT DO *BOXERS* TAKE TO KEEP *HEALTHY?*

... *FIGHT*-AMINS!

WHAT DID THE *CRITIC* SAY ABOUT THE *NEW OUTER SPACE RESTAURANT?*

... "THE FOOD WAS GOOD BUT THERE WAS NO *ATMOSPHERE!*"

What do you call someone who sings songs about the moon?

A lunar crooner!

WHY DID THE *TULIP* GO TO THE *DOCTOR?*

... IT HAD HIGH *BUD* PRESSURE!

Yoe!

WHY DID THE *STOMACH* FEEL *BEATEN* UP?
... FIRST IT GOT A *PAUNCH,* THEN A *BELT!*

WHAT KIND OF *TRUCK* DOES A *FROG* DRIVE?
... A *TOAD* TRUCK!

WHAT DO **YOU** CALL A **MAN** WHO WORKS IN THE **ALPHABET SOUP FACTORY?**

... A MAN OF **LETTERS!**

WHAT KIND OF **PERSON** MAKES A GOOD **JOKE WRITER?**

... THE DOWN TO **MIRTH** TYPE!

What do you call a really happy bird?

A perky turkey!

WHAT DID ONE **HAMBURGER PATTY** SAY TO THE OTHER **HAMBURGER PATTY?**

... "WE'RE **ON A ROLL!**"

MICK: WHAT WAS THE **50TH STATE?**
RICK: **HAWAII!**
MICK: I'M FINE, **HAWAII** YOU?

WHAT IS A *CHEERLEADER'S* FAVORITE *CAR?*

... AN ACU-*RAH-RAH!*

HOW *OLD* IS YOUR *GRANDMOTHER?*

... I DON'T KNOW, BUT WE'VE *HAD* HER FOR A *LONG TIME!*

WHY DID THE *SILLY NASCAR DRIVER* MAKE SO MANY *PIT STOPS?*

... HE KEPT ASKING FOR *DIRECTIONS!*

Oh, no... it's The Moe & Joe Show! ® *Moe:* Say, Joe! What does a big ape use to defende herself?

 Joe: Well, Moe... Kong-fu!

What do you call a dock where boats are parked?

A yacht lot!

ARE **YOU** SURE THERE AREN'T ANY **SHARKS** AROUND **HERE?**

... YES, THE **ALLIGATORS** SCARED THEM **AWAY!**

HAT HAS **FANGS** AND IS **WAITING** FOR YOU AT **4:00?**

... AN AFTER SCHOOL **SNAKE!**

WHAT IS A *MUSIC TEACHER'S* FAVORITE *DRINK?*

... COCA-COLA-*LA-LA-LA!*

WHAT DO *YOU* GET WHEN YOU CROSS *POULTRY* WITH *STAR TREK?*

... CHICKEN *SPOCKS!*

Oh, no... it's **The Moe & Joe Show!** ® *Moe*: Say, Joe! What is a scarecrow's favorite fruit?

 Joe: Well, Moe... straw-berries!

WHAT DOES A *POLICE OFFICER* EAT
AT THE *MOVIES?*

... *COP*-CORN!

WHAT DO *ASTRONAUTS* BRING TO THE
SCHOOL CAFETERIA?

... *LAUNCH* MONEY!

WHAT DO *VEGETABLES* USE TO SEND
OVERNIGHT PACKAGES?

... UNITED *PARSLEY* SERVICE!

Oh, no... it's **The Moe & Joe Show!** ® *Moe*: Say, Joe! Where did the robber eat lunch?

 Joe: Well, Moe... Burglar King!

WHY DON'T *HIPPOS* JOIN THE *BOY SCOUTS?*
... THEY DON'T LOOK *GOOD* IN *GREEN!*

What do you get when you make your father angry?

A mad dad!

What do you call it when all of the monkeys leave the zoo?

An ape escape!

WHAT DO *YOU* GET WHEN YOU CROSS YOUR *TASTE BUDS* WITH A *TORNADO?*

... A *TONGUE* TWISTER!

WHY DIDN'T *CLARK KENT* WALK *UNDER* THE *LADDER?*

 ... HE WAS *SUPER*-STITIOUS!

WHAT IS A *DOG DOCTOR'S* FAVORITE *CAR?*

... A COR-*VET!*

WHAT IS A *SINGER'S* FAVORITE *FOOD?*

... *HUM*-BURGERS!

BILL: I HAD A *PART* IN A *MOVIE* CALLED "*BREAKFAST* WITH *MELVIN!*"
LIL: DID YOU HAVE A BIG *ROLE?*
BILL: NO, JUST A *BOWL* OF *CEREAL!*

RHYME TIME!

What do you call a boy who's nervous around girls?

A shy guy!

WHAT IS A **SKUNK'S** FAVORITE **SNACK?**

... **STENCH** FRIES

WHAT DOES A **KANGAROO** EAT AT THE **MOVIES?**

... **HOP**-CORN!

What do you get when you buy a lot of pickles?

A dill bill!

WHY DID THE *GRAPE* KISS THE *BANANA?*

... BECAUSE IT HAD *A-PEEL!*

WHAT IS *GREEN*, WEIGHS *6,000 POUNDS*, AND GOES *"RIBBIT, RIBBIT?"*

... TWO *3,000 POUND FROGS!*

Oh, no... it's **The Moe & Joe Show!** ® **Moe**: Say, Joe! What kind of motorcycle did Attila drive?

Joe: Well, Moe... a Hun-dai!

What do you call a contest that gives away ceramics?

A pottery lottery!

WHAT DID THE *ARTIST* DO WHEN HE WAS A *BABY*?

... HE *DREW*-LED!

WHAT DO *RADIATORS* EAT AT A *MEXICAN RESTAURANT*?

... FA-*HEAT*-AS!

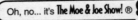 Oh, no... it's **The Moe & Joe Show!** ® *Moe*: Say, Joe! What does a dog eat at the movies?

 Joe: Well, Moe... pup-corn!

WHAT KIND OF **MONEY** DOES A **SNOWMAN** HAVE?

... **COLD CASH!**

WHAT'S SO **UNUSUAL** ABOUT THE **INVISIBLE MAN?**

... WELL, YOU DON'T **SEE** ONE EVERY DAY!

WHERE DO **BABY TREES** GO TO **SCHOOL?**

... A **NURSERY!**

Oh, no... it's **The Moe & Joe Show!** ®

 Moe: Say, Joe! What is a thirsty person's favorite snack?

 Joe: Well, Moe... quench fries!

WHY DID THE POISON IVY GET INTO TROUBLE?
... BECAUSE SHE WAS ACTING RASH!

WHAT HAPPENED WHEN THE STRAWBERRIES GOT INTO A CAR ACCIDENT?
... THEY CAUSED A TRAFFIC JAM!

WHAT DO YOU CALL AN ELEPHANT WITH CURLY HAIR?
... A PACHY-PERM!

What happens if a monkey breaks his leg?

A chimp limp!

WHERE DO *PIGS* KEEP THEIR *DIRTY CLOTHES?*

... IN THE *HAM*-PER

WHAT KIND OF *KEYS* DOES A *BAKER* USE TO START HIS *CAR?*

... COO-*KEYS!*

WHAT HAPPENED TO THE **CROOK** WHO **ROBBED** THE **LAUNDROMAT?**

... HE MADE A **CLEAN** GETAWAY!

ANN: IF YOUR **SHOES** WERE A **FRUIT,** WHAT **FRUIT** WOULD THEY **BE?**
STAN: A **PEAR!**

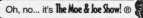 Oh, no... it's **The Moe & Joe Show!** ® **Moe:** Say, Joe! Why don't mummies get married?

 Joe: Well, Moe... because they have cold feet!

 HY DID THE **BOOK** YELL IN THE **AIRPORT?**

... HE WAS **PAGE**-ING PEOPLE.

WHAT'S IN YOUR **POCKET** WHEN IT'S **EMPTY?**

 ... A **HOLE!**

WHAT DOES **SANTA CLAUS** EAT AT A **MEXICAN RESTAURANT?**

... **CHIMNEY**-CHANGAS!

Oh, no... it's **The Moe & Joe Show!** ® **Moe:** Say, Joe! What is a choirmaster's favorite food?

 Joe: Well, Moe... hymn-burgers!

WHAT IS A DOG'S *LEAST* FAVORITE *BREATH MINT?*

... *TICK* TACS!

WOMAN: I SEE YOU'RE BUILDING A *NEW* HOUSE!
CARPENTER: THAT'S THE *ONLY* KIND WE *BUILD!*

What do you call warm weather in the winter time?

Snow foe!

WHAT **LETTER** IS **HARD** OF **HEARING?**

... **A!**

WHAT DO **YOU** CALL A **CAT** THAT **JUMPS** FROM THE **MANTLE** TO THE **FLOOR?**

... **HI-LOW** KITTY!

JANE: WHY DO *YOU* HAVE THAT *HAMBURGER* ON YOUR *HEAD?*
SHANE: *OH, NO!* I MUST HAVE *EATEN* MY *HAT* FOR *DINNER!*

WHY DID THE *TEACHER* GO TO THE *EYE DOCTOR?*

... SHE HAD PROBLEMS WITH HER *PUPILS!*

HAT DID THE *WOODSMAN* HAVE AFTER HE GOT NEW *GLASSES?*

... *AX*-RAY VISION

 Oh, no... it's **The Moe & Joe Show!** ® **Moe:** Say, Joe! What is a repairman's favorite snack?

 Joe: Well, Moe... wrench fries!

WHAT DO **YOU** CALL **SPAGHETTI** THAT **MAKES FUN** OF PEOPLE?

... **MOCK**-ARONI!

Where does the king of skeletons sit?

A bone throne!